ISBN-13: 978-0615950037
ISBN-10: 0615950035
Published by Create Space an Amazon Co.

All Scripture quotations are taken from Bible
Gateway. Web. 25 Oct. 2012.

Printed in the United States of America

Special Thanks

I would like to start by saying thank you to God who has empowered and graced me to write this book. I and my family are where we are today because of God's favor and blessings on our life; to God be the Gory.

To my incredible wife, Marquita: Marquita, you are the greatest gift God has given to me. I am such a blessed and happy man with you by my side. Your support and cheers mean the world to me. I love you.

To my graphic designer and brother, Jeremiah: Jeremiah, I owe you big. The long hours and dedicated work that you put in for this project was more than I can compensate you for, Thank you for being patient with me through all of my many changes. You're the BEST!

To the greatest church family in the entire world, Life Church International: LCI, I am extremely proud to be your pastor and leader. You all have matured me and blessed my family in so many countless ways. You all are always my number one supporters and biggest fans in everything I do. I See Life!

To my family: Dad, Overseer B. E. Williams, Mother, Lady La'Trice Williams and Grandmothers, Earnestine Williams and Constance Herring. Thank you all for your love, wisdom and support. When all else fails family is always there to see you through. Family is God's gift to each of us.

To my babies, Navah, Jade and Marcellas: Thank you three for being my motivation and inspiration. Daddy really appreciates your sacrifices and love. I love you all!

Exordium

Although we live in a day and season where fiscal concerns and financial subjects seem to dominate the front pages of the Wall Street Journal, USA Today and many other prominent periodicals, the Body of Christ is not worried, but preparing itself for the great wealth of God.

Reason, there are no famines in the kingdom of God's people. Specifically, since we see financial challenges as an opportunity for God to express and manifest His wonders among us ~ the people of God. Our fiduciary responsibilities will be met as a result of seed sowing, budgeting and wise spending habits that are preached, taught and strongly emphasized from our pulpits and mid-week services. No longer does the twenty-first century church teach/preach the traditional sermons, but we are mindful to insert the everyday operational principles that are necessary for a whole means of living and progression.

The Word of God declares it is He who gives us the power to get wealth, thus Christians are determined and convinced that all of our answers are documented in the Holy Writ, and our directives are hidden in the golden nuggets of the Scriptures. Wealth is laced all throughout biblical text and mentioned as "*...money answereth all things*" (Eccl. 10:19).

As a twenty-first century warrior springing forth with knowledge, Pastor J. Marcellas Williams presents the wealth of God for the Body of Christ in practicality and easy written form. He shares principles of wealth, personal testimonies and strategies for our current day and future in the prosperity of God.

Our days of poverty are over and done with due to our knowledge of the wealth in God's divine principles. As members of the Christian faith we are encouraged and challenged to tithe, sow seed, give offerings and first fruits according to the Scriptures, and it is all done via faith and obedience. This book "WEALTH ON PURPOSE" highlights that your present and future riches are not just a "pie in the sky", but a direct lineage to your practice of God's curriculum that will set our journey toward the continuance of God's financial blessing.

Set your mindset for greatness and plan your agenda for success on various levels, but it will only happen when you take time to read, digest and study written materials like this published work that will guide you in the ideology of God's wealth. MONEY KNOWS MONEY AND IS COMING IN OUR DIRECTION.

Bishop Eric D. Garnes, D.Min, MPS
Presiding Prelate, United Covenant Churches of Christ
Senior Pastor, Tabernacle of Praise (Cathedral)
Brooklyn, New York

Foreword

You may have read books or attended conferences on the topic before--but not like this one. **"Wealth On Purpose"** is not just an instruction manual. It is a pastor's recommendation on how to assess your wealth using qualities that are neglected by many Christians today. Through these teachings that I've been privy to sit under and learn as a pastor myself, I have seen them work if they are properly adhered to and applied.

I've seen and heard the testimonies of persons who have diligently walked out these principles. Lives have been changed and made better financially only after becoming good stewards over what God has already given. The Word of God is true....He has given us the power to get wealth (Deut. 8:18). This is foundational teaching in which I highly recommend. This teaching belongs in the hands of every person, especially every believer who seeks and prays for financial reformation. It's a MUST!!!!

Curtis C. Johnson
Founder-Pastor, The Perfecting Saints Church,
Jacksonville, Fl.

Table of Contents

Testimonials

Wealth on Purpose
Budget Spreadsheet

TO SECURE YOUR
BUDGET
SPREADSHEET ON USB
OR EMAIL PLEASE
CONTACT
J MARCELLAS
ENITERPRISE:
jmarcellasw@gmail.com
or (904) 765-9224
P.O. BOX 3347
JACKSONVILLE, FL
32206

Salutation

Greetings,

Thank you for supporting and investing into J. Marcellas Ministries and into your own life and ministry. What an honor it is to be used by God as a vessel to compose this book. The greatest revelry for me is to hear the countless testimonies that have been birthed as a result of God's people applying the principles shared within this book. The first testimony came from my own struggles that were turned into victories. By using these principles I live a financially free life enjoying the wealth of God in every area of my life. I will also be the first to say although the principles and teachings in this handbook are simple and easy to understand and apply, habits are hard to break. Bad habits are broken when bad thinking is fixed. This book will challenge and cause a change from bad thinking to discerning God's way as it relates to finances.

I serve as the pastor and founder of Life Church International of Jacksonville, Florida. God has blessed the LCI family tremendously since its inception in 2007. I also assist as the Adjutant Chaplain to the Presiding Bishop of the United Covenant Churches of Christ, Bishop Eric D. Garnes. In addition, I currently succor patients and families as a Chaplain at University of Florida Health at Jacksonville. My most joyful and rewarding area of service I render as unto God is being a husband to my wife and a father to my children. I am proudly married to Marquita Denise Williams since October 1, 2006. She is my rock and my love. She is my parenting partner to our three children, Navah Simone, Jade Michelle and Marcellas Dominic.

Once more, thank you for your support. I am excited about your future. Be sure to pray and seek God before and while reading and working through this book. Ask God to speak to you and reveal to you his Word and instructions for your life through this work.

Peace and Prosperity,
Pastor J. Marcellas Williams
Founder/Pastor, Life Church International
Jacksonville, FL

Confession

Start first by grabbing an item that represents income flowing into your life. (E.g. wallet, purse, debit/credit card etc.) Now, while clutching this item, recite the following confession aloud.

God takes pleasure in my prosperity! Therefore, the cycle of poverty has been broken from my life. I have financial discipline. God can trust me with wealth. I no longer live with holes in my pockets. For I have blessed pockets. Therefore, I give and I live in Wealth on Purpose, in Jesus' name, Amen!

Wealth on Purpose Overview

Prosperity is not a money message it's an obedience message. Money gives you recognition with God and man. So it is important as a Christian we understand how to manage money. Being wealthy is the result of exercising the principles of managing money. Wealth is not gained by winning the lottery, inheriting a large amount of cash or an estate, making a good investment or having a high paying job. All these examples only produce you money, not wealth. I know you may say, 'well that's good enough for me'. However, money in the hands of a fool or a financially unlearned person will quickly vanish and not easily return. Managing well the money you have is when wealth is accomplished.

The Bible states that God takes pleasure in seeing his children prosper. (Psalm 35:27)

Therefore, the opposing thought to this scripture is that God grieves when His children live in poverty. It is not God's will for your life that you should live poor and struggling. God has called you to be the head, the leader, the light and the example. Christians do a splendid job of showing an example of being poverty stricken holy rollers, but we do a poor job of being an example of living well and prosperous as children in the Kingdom of God should.

Yes, having wealth on purpose requires discipline and time, but most of all it demands a change of mindset. You must change the way you think about money and God. You can change your life by changing your mind. Let's exercise your mind now. Please take a moment now and turn back to the Wealth on Purpose Confession on page 8 and proclaim the confession aloud. Make it a practice to recite this confession every day. The more you say it the more you will believe it; the more you believe it the more you will walk in it.

I will teach you according to the word of God **5 Principles of Giving**, **4 Steps to Wealth**, **8 Laws of Wealth** and **7 On Purpose Steps**. Then I will share several real life testimonials attained from lessons learned in this book. Let us begin with simply listing the **5 Principles of Giving** with a brief introduction of each principle. Then a more in depth study to follow.

5 Principles of Giving

1) First Fruit: God teaches his children to allow Him to be at the forefront of everything we do. The beginning of every year we are commanded to sow the amount of one week's salary in the Kingdom (the church). When we make this deposit into the Kingdom, God secures blessings over our finances for the entire year. The key is to start off with God and permit Him to carry you instead of you trying to carry yourself. I know it sounds bizarre and radical; however it is a practical principle of life. If you do not start properly, then you will not end properly. For example, when buttoning a shirt, if you button the first button out of place then the rest of the shirt will be out of alignment resulting in you looking a mess. See how simple that is! I will give you more help with First Fruit later. Let's go to the next principle for now.

2) Tithe: God desires to have a father to child love relationship with us. He is not after our money. He

owns everything and does not need our money or money at all. He is pursuing our heart. Tithing is taught all throughout the Bible in the Old and New Testaments. Therefore, it is still relevant and necessary. God explained to the Children of Israel that they had been disobedient and have walked away from their relationship with Him. He then makes a deal with them. He proposes, if they returned back to Him that He would return back unto them. The Children of Israel were interested in the deal and asked God how they could return. God then began to talk about money and tithing. Some say that God never answered their question because He started talking about money.

Let me explain. God really wanted to know where their hearts were. Jesus teaches us in the New Testament that wherever your treasure or money is, is where your heart resides. So God instructs us to not only verbalize that we love Him, but to show Him through tithing. You do not have to display your love on a banner or use a megaphone to express it. I can take a look at your bank statement and tell you who and what you love. Tithing is about having a love relationship with God and acknowledging that He is the source of all you have. Whew! It is a bit much to take in, I understand. No worries, I will help you comprehend it even better later. Let me introduce you to the next principle.

3) Shepherd's Seed:

Unfortunately, there have been far too many of our Christian leaders who have given the church a bad reputation concerning the subject of money. Some have raped and manipulated people out of money. This growing epidemic is a disgrace to the body of Christ. It does not represent the Word of God or the Christ we serve. On the other hand, there are other Christian leaders who are God sent and sincerely care for God's people and humankind in general. These men and women of God are very important for your life and living. Do you have a Pastor, a Covering, or a Shepard in your life? If not, then ask God to send you to one. Sorry, but the famous and popular televangelists do not qualify as your Pastor.

You need a Leader who knows you and one that you can reach out to when you need him. You are not an island. You cannot make it through this life on your own. God has assigned a Pastor to you to cover you in prayer, watch over your soul, guide you in the things of God and challenge you to be a better you. We can never adequately compensate our leaders for what they mean to our lives. However, God does ask us to sow into their lives.

This financial seed is different from the first two mentioned, in that God puts a specified dollar amount on First Fruit and Tithe. For the Shepard's seed God only asks us to give something consistently to our leader. The reward is that when we take care of our spiritual leader God, as a result, will supply all of our needs. You will find this teaching in Philippians 4:19. Be careful to read the whole chapter. When you do you will realize this promise from God does not apply to everyone. It only applies to those who take care of the man or woman of God assigned to their life. Let's pause here. I only wanted to arouse your appetite for you to be hungry to explore more into this principle. We will unpack more of this in a moment.

4) Kingdom Giving: The Kingdom Giving principle refers to offerings. Most people are familiar with offering, but if not, it is when the congregants give a freewill monetary donation to the church. God promises that when we give it will come back to us in abundance – the law of reciprocity. God says in Malachi chapter three that we have robbed him in tithe and offering. In order to activate the law of reciprocity in your offerings you must be mindful of two prerequisites.

First, you must give your tithe. The tithe does not belong to you, it belongs to God. So to try and give an offering and expect a return after you have withheld the tithe, thus stolen from God, will never work. First thing is first. Tithing is the cover charge for access into heaven's storeroom of blessings. Once you are in then you may give an offering. Giving an offering is making an investment. The more you invest the better your return will be.

Secondly, you have to have the right attitude and approach. The Bible declares that God loves a cheerful giver. It also instructs not to give grudgingly. If our attitude and our heart posture is wrong toward God, the church or our leaders then God will refuse our offering. In other words, you may donate the money and the entity you donated to will deposit it, but if your attitude is obscene in your giving, God will not acknowledge it. Consequently, you will not receive a return. We see this example in Genesis. Cain killed Abel as a result of God refusing Cain's offering, but accepting Abel's. Cain and his offering were rejected due to his attitude toward God and the offering. Very interesting story, we will come back to this transitorily.

5) Alms Giving: My father always says, "It's just nice to be nice." Alms Giving is being genuinely nice, giving and kind to people. God desires to use people on earth to be his hands, feet, mouth etc. We

are extensions of God's love in a tangible way. This kind of generosity is benevolence to the poor and the least. This requires selflessness. You give without expecting anything in return from the one you gave to. You do not go and brag on it and expose the other person's misfortune. Your reward will come from God alone. When we give to the poor we are giving to God.

Now buckle up and take this journey with me as we study the 5 Principles of Giving together a slight more in depth.

5 Principles of Giving

1) **First Fruit**

2) Tithe

3) Shepherd's Seed

4) Kingdom Giving

5) Alms Giving

Hebrew meaning: the first, the beginning, the principle thing

Greek meaning: a beginning of sacrifice

<u>Principle</u>: If the beginning is blessed the rest is blessed (Romans 11:16 KJV *For if the firstfruit be holy, the lump is also holy: and if the root be holy so are the branches.)*

<u>Purpose</u>: Honor the Lord first and He shall fill you with plenty until it overflows (Proverbs 3:9-10 GWT *Honor the LORD with your wealth and with the first and best part of all your income. Then your barns will be full, and your vats will overflow with fresh wine.)*

<u>Prohibition</u>: Don't tamper with it. It is holy to the Lord (Ezekiel 48:14 KJV *And they shall not*

sell of it, neither exchange, nor alienate the
firstfruits of the land: for it is holy unto the LORD.)

Place: **In the house of God** (Exodus 23:19 KJV
The first of the firstfruits of thy land thou shalt bring
into the house of the LORD thy God. Thou shalt not
seethe a kid in his mother's milk.)

Priest: **Reserved to help care for the priests**

– The priest shall cause the blessing to rest
in your house (Ezekiel 44:30 KJV *And the first of*
all the firstfruits of all things, and every oblation of
all, of every sort of your oblations, shall be the
priest's: ye shall also give unto the priest the first of
your dough, that he may cause the blessing to rest
in thine house.)

– Helps to keep your priest encouraged (2
Chronicles 31:4 KJV *Moreover he commanded the*
people that dwelt in Jerusalem to give the portion of
the priests and the Levites, that they might be
encouraged in the law of the LORD.)

Practice: **It consists of a fourth of your monthly**
income. This amount is to be ideally presented to

God at the beginning of each year. However, whenever you activate this principle it will work for you. The cycle of harvesting in the Bible days was first to sow a seed, next maintain the ground and seed and finally harvest the crop. Our cycle today is still the same. We start a job, a business or receive a monthly check, (i.e. SSI, Disability, Alimony, Child Support etc.) next we work the job or business and finally we collect an income. In the time when agriculture was the trade of the day their time of harvest would vary depending on what seed was planted. For us today in America our time of seed and harvest is calculated on an every thirty day increment. In other words, our harvest is based on a month's income. For example, if you are trying to get a car loan the financing company will ask you to show proof of your income from the last thirty days. You may ask, how do I calculate what the amount of my First Fruit will be? Our thirty day periods are divided into four weeks. So your First Fruit amount will be the sum total of one week. You calculate what you make for thirty days and divide by four and that gives you your First Fruit amount that you present to God. Through this act of obedience you say to God I acknowledge that you are the giver of all I have and I desire to place you first in every area of my life. In return, God allows the principle of the First Fruit to cover your entire year. Consequently, your financial makeup for the whole year will be blessed and covered by God.

For illustration, let's say you make $1000 every thirty days. When you dived that by four (which represents four weeks) you get $250. As a result, $250 is your First Fruit amount.

Your Pay - $1000 per month / by 4 =

Your First Fruit - $250

As you progress throughout the year, and you receive a steady raise in your income, you are to give God the first of the raise. Let's continue our illustration. You are already receiving $1000 per thirty days and you have given the First Fruit amount of $250 and now it is six months later and you receive a steady raise in your income from

$1000 to $1100. You now receive $100 more per thirty days. You take the $100 and divide by four (which represents four weeks) and you $25. This becomes your First Fruit that you give one time.

Your Raise – **$100 more per month / by 4 =**

Your First Fruit - **$25**

So here is what has happened, you were obedient and gave your First Fruit and God in return blessed you and honored you by giving you a raise because you honored Him by showing Him that all you have belongs to Him. This cycle of gaining and increasing continues as you are obedient in your First Fruit.

Harvesting is the process of gathering what has grown from the seeds sown. The harvest marks the end of the growing cycle. On small farms with minimal mechanization, harvesting is the most labor intensive activity of the growing season. On large, mechanized farms, harvesting utilizes the most expensive and sophisticated farm machinery. There are a number of actions required after removing the crops: cooling, sorting, cleaning, packing, processing and shipping. Receiving is not the end; it's the beginning of responsibility of being blessed. When God blesses you with a harvest or income (increase, blessing) it requires you to take responsible action. We show God we are grateful or ungrateful by the type of steward we are of what He blesses us with.

Hindrance – There are contingencies to receiving the blessings of God. Here are four concepts to keep in mind and in your life in order to receive the blessings of God. If you do not keep these, you will hinder your progress and growth. The bases of these concepts are derived from the following scripture. (Matthew 6:33 KJV *But seek ye first the kingdom of God, and his righteousness: and all these things shall be added unto you.*)

- Know the ways of the Kingdom of God
- Trust the God of the Kingdom
- Live according to His ways
- Good stuff comes as a result of good living

NOTES

_____

_____

_____

_____

_____

_____

_____

_____

_____

_____

_____

_____

_____

_____

_____

> "It is not the creation of wealth that is wrong, but the love of money for its own sake."
>
> — Margaret Thatcher

5 Principles of Giving

1) First Fruit

2) **Tithe**

3) Shepherd's Seed

4) Kingdom Giving

5) Alms Giving

Foundation: *Leviticus 27:30 KJV And all the tithe of the land, whether of the seed of the land, or of the fruit of the tree, is the Lord's: it is **holy** unto the Lord.*

Example: Abram tithes to Melchizedek (*Genesis 14:18-20 And Melchizedek king of Salem brought forth bread and wine: and he was the priest of the most high God. And he blessed him, and said, Blessed be Abram of the most high God, possessor of heaven and earth: And blessed be the most high God, which hath delivered thine enemies into thy hand. And he gave him tithes of all.*)

Amount: Each year you are to set aside a **tenth (10%) of all the produce** grown in your fields.

(Deuteronomy 14:22 *Thou shalt truly tithe all the increase of thy seed, that the field bringeth forth year by year.*)

Purpose: 1) God desires a sincere heart to heart relationship between himself and his children. God does not need our money, He longs for our heart and our obedience.

(Malachi 3:6-8 *For I am the LORD, I change not; therefore ye sons of Jacob are not consumed. Even from the days of your fathers ye are gone away from mine ordinances, and have not kept them. Return unto me, and I will return unto you, saith the LORD of hosts. But ye said, wherein shall we return?*) *Will a man rob God? Yet ye have robbed me. But ye say, wherein have we robbed thee? In tithes and offerings.*

The above scriptures shows a Father that is grieving because his children have disobeyed him and walked off from the relationship they once had with him. This heartbroken father exclaims their rebellion and then pleads with them to return to him and as a result he would return to them. The children accept the offer and ask how they can return. The father seemingly switches subjects and starts talking about money. However, he is actually still talking about relationship. The father understands the principle of the heart which is explained in Matthew 6:21 *For where your treasure is, there will your heart be also.* The father in essence explains that he will know where their heart is by what they do with their money.

2) God has designed the tithe to furnish the needs of the local church.

(Malachi 3:10 *Bring ye all the tithes into the storehouse, that there may be meat in mine house...)*

The tithe has a mission attached to it. It is to support the budget and expenses of the church. The church is then commissioned to utilize these funds to support the staff, facilities, and utilities. Most importantly extend themselves outside of their four walls and use the same funds to take care of the hungry, poor, homeless and less fortunate.

3) God has designed the tithe to give us access to the abundance of riches and blessings in heaven.

(Malachi 3:10-12 *...and prove me now herewith, saith the LORD of hosts, if I will not open you the windows of heaven, and pour you out a blessing, that there shall not be room enough to receive it. And I will rebuke the devourer for your sakes, and he shall not destroy the fruits of your ground; neither shall your vine cast her fruit before the time in the field, saith the LORD of hosts. And all nations shall call you blessed: for ye shall be a delightsome land, saith the LORD of hosts.*)

This is what I describe as the 8 Fold Blessing that God has promised to every believer. See next page.

8 Fold Blessing
Tithe and Offering

1) Windows of heaven are open to you

2) God will pour out a blessing to you

3) The blessing will be in overflow

4) God will hold back the enemy from you

5) Your blessings shall not be destroyed

6) God will ensure you don't birth prematurely

7) The glory/favor of God will shine on you

8) People will sow into your life perpetually

Malachi 3:10-12

How it works: Tithing is a sign of respect, gratitude and acknowledgement toward God. Tithing is our reasonable service. Tithing affords us access to the promise not complete fulfillment of the promise. Consider the example below. It is quite unorthodox so brace yourself!

All Saints Strip Club

I used the All Saints Strip Club as an example to demonstrate the principles of tithing and giving.

Like any strip club there is a cover fee you must pay in order to enter the establishment. Once you are in the club you observe all of the wonders of the strip club. Gorgeous people are everywhere for your pleasure. Tonight is featuring: Sasha, Delicious, Candy, Too Thick, Brown Sugar and Chocolate Surprise. The amenities include: lap dances out on the main floor. Also, there is the V.I.P room where you can enjoy the night in an upscale exclusive room. The first three drinks are on the house and you can have any dancer you desire to accompany you. In the Red Light Room you will find a private enclosed area guarded by a bouncer for forty five minutes with any dancer that will agree. Each service comes with a separate fee with the V.I.P room costing more than a lap dance and the Red Light Room costing the most. All of these great enjoyments are at your disposal but you cannot access them unless you pay an EXTRA fee. Yes, you are in the building but paying the cover charge only will not award you any of the advantages. You have to invest more to partake in all that the club has to offer.

The same is true regarding tithe and offering. Paying your tithe is your cover charge where God allows you into His Kingdom where there is an endless list of virtues that you can partake in. However, your tithe (cover charge) only affords you entrance. It is a sign of respect and acknowledgement to the owner-God. Much like the club, you pay the cover charge instead of sneaking in. This shows your respect to the owner. Moreover, it is your offering that causes God to acquiesce you to enjoy the offered extravagances from the Kingdom of God. The more you freely give the more you receive. The Bible teaches that God will give back to you his measure of abundance when you are obedient in giving.

Top 10 Reasons People Do not Tithe

10. Stingy

9. They don't trust the church

8. Poor money management

7. Believes that giving 10% of their time and talent takes the place of giving money

6. Believes it is a money scheme concocted by the pastor

5. Says tithing has never worked for them

4. Living from check to check is satisfactory

3. Fear of not having enough money to pay bills

2. No real understanding of the true meaning and purpose of tithing

1. They don't trust God

NOTES

"Being wealthy is the result of exercising the principles of managing money."

~ J. Marcellas ~

5 Principles of Giving

1) First Fruit

2) Tithe

3) **Shepherd's Seed**

4) Kingdom Giving

5) Alms Giving

Resource: It is biblically supported that the Pastor should be supported financially by the church. Apostle Paul explains plainly in the scriptures below.

(1 Corinthians 9: 3-14 MSG *I'm not shy in standing up to my critics. We who are on missionary assignments for God have a right to decent accommodations, and we have a right to support for us and our families. You don't seem to have raised questions with the other apostles and our Master's brothers and Peter in these matters. So, why me? Is it just Barnabas and I who have to go it alone and pay our own way? Are soldiers self-employed? Are gardeners forbidden to eat vegetables from their own gardens? Don't milkmaids get to drink their fill from the pail? I'm not just sounding off because I'm irritated. This is all written in the scriptural law.*

SEE PAGES 46 AND 47 TO WRITE NOTES FOR THIS SECTION

Moses wrote, "Don't muzzle an ox to keep it from eating the grain when it's threshing." Do you think Moses' primary concern was the care of farm animals? Don't you think his concern extends to us? Of course. Farmers plow and thresh expecting something when the crop comes in. So if we have planted spiritual seed among you, is it out of line to expect a meal or two from you? Others demand plenty from you in these ways. Don't we who have never demanded deserve even more? But we're not going to start demanding now what we've always had a perfect right to. Our decision all along has been to put up with anything rather than to get in the way or detract from the Message of Christ. All I'm concerned with right now is that you not use our decision to take advantage of others, depriving them of what is rightly theirs. You know, don't you, that it's always been taken for granted that those who work in the Temple live off the proceeds of the Temple, and that those who offer sacrifices at the altar eat their meals from what has been sacrificed? Along the same lines, the Master directed that those who spread the Message be supported by those who believe the Message.)

Responsibility: It is a biblical response for the receivers of the Word to bless the giver of the Word.

(Galatians 6: 6, 9 [6] Those who are taught the word of God should provide for their teachers, sharing all good things with them. [9] So let's not get tired of doing what is good. At just the right time we will reap a harvest of blessing if we don't give up.)

Recipe: God is a cause and effect God.

Cause – you supplied the needs of your pastor.

Effect – God provides your needs.

Here are two scriptures to help us understand this revelation.

2 Corinthians 9:7 (Every man according as he purposeth in his heart, so let him give; not grudgingly, or of necessity: for God loveth a cheerful giver.)

Philippians 4:19 (*But my God shall supply all your need according to his riches in glory by Christ Jesus.*)

God teaches us through the writings of Paul that we are not to give out of necessity or because we have needs. Although, it is widely taught that if you have a need then sow a seed (it should be said that if you have a desire sow a seed); this is only half correct. God has a specific avenue from which your need may be met. The avenue is through your Leader/Pastor. The commonly quoted scripture Philippians 4:19 that gives a promise of God supplying all of your need is aimed to a specific group of people. This chapter in Philippians (please read chapter 4 in its entirety) starts by Paul showing his appreciation to the church of Philippi for taking care of him and sending him provision for his needs when no other church would. He goes further to admonish the church to continue sending gifts and finances to him, but not so that he could gain. He explains he has learned how to have and how not to have and be content in both. However, Paul urges them to continue giving to him so that their gifts will be accounted to them by God. Moreover, Paul provides incentive for them to carry on in their manner of giving by promising them that as they supply his need that God will supply their need. The individuals he was referring to were only those who had taken care of him. As a result, when you take care of your Leader/Pastor then God will supply all of your need. If you do not, then this promise does not work for you. There is no specified amount to give to your Pastor, so the principle that the more you give the more you receive applies.

NOTES

_____

_____

_____

_____

_____

"Virtue does not come from wealth, but...
Wealth and every other good thing which men have...comes from virtue."

~ Socrates ~

5 Principles of Giving

1) First Fruit

2) Tithe

3) Shepherd's Seed

4) **Kingdom Giving**

5) Alms Giving

<u>**Rule**</u>**: You must invest in order to expect a return**.

Luke 6:38 (*Give, and it shall be given unto you; good measure, pressed down, and shaken together, and running over, shall men give into your bosom. For with the same measure that ye mete withal it shall be measured to you again.*)

This rule is a principle of life that is true and applies in every walk of life. For example, my wife and I have three children and we are intentional about investing in them. We invest our love, time and affection in them. We also invest education and faith in them. In return, we have children that value family and enjoy intimate family time. They are kids who show love, respect and compassion toward themselves and others. They are also accomplished in their schooling and strong in their spiritual faith. These favorable results from our children that my wife and I experience are a direct result of the intentional investments we have made. We expect nothing less because the more time, love and affection, education and faith we invest the better the result.

The same applies to money and God. When you give to God you are making an investment into your financial future. When you give it will be given back to you, but according to the above scripture in Luke, what comes back to you is actually more than what you gave. I like to call it the Law of Reciprocity-PLUS. According to Clairvoyant, Spirit-Medium, Intuitive Healer and Spiritual Coach *Amirah:* "The Law of Reciprocity means: to give and take mutually; to return in kind or even in another kind of degree". Therefore, Reciprocity-PLUS is when not only do you get back what you gave but you get back a surplus, over and beyond what you have given. This is the promise that God gives to Kingdom givers. If you are experiencing any form of financial stress or lack right now then your remedy is kingdom giving or sowing seeds. Your participation in doing things God's way is a matter of your level of trust in Him. He is aware of all you are going through and desperately wants to help you out of distress and usher you into great blessings. Yet, God patiently awaits your permission before he moves in your life. We must trust God's instructions and be careful to obey them.

Terms and Conditions: You control the rate of return. *2 Corinthians 9:6-8* (*Remember this: Whoever sows sparingly will also reap sparingly, and whoever sows generously will also reap generously. Each man should give what he has decided in his heart to give, not reluctantly or under compulsion, for God loves a cheerful giver. And God is able to make all grace abound to you, so that in all things at all times, having all that you need, you will abound in every good work.*)

This passage explains your rate of return. If you give to God and people only small sporadic amounts, then that is what you will receive in return. On the contrary, when you give much more and often, then you will receive much more and often. You must learn how to budget your money so you are not always giving on impulse and not taking care of your responsibilities. However, there will be times where God will ask you to give spontaneously or rather when you have not planned to do so and even when it may seem as if you cannot afford to do so. During these unplanned prompts by the Holy Spirit for you to give is when you need to only be obedient and not try and logically figure it out. Only trust God because this is when He is up to something big in return for you. Remember, obedience is always better than sacrifice.

2 Corinthians 9:10-11 (*Now he who supplies seed to the sower and bread for food will also supply and increase your store of seed and will enlarge the harvest of your righteousness. You will be made rich in every way so that you can be generous on every occasion, and through us your generosity will result in thanksgiving to God.*)

I like the above passage because it offers incentive to be a sower or giver. The scripture explicates that

God continuously provides substance to those He can trust will give. For when you decide to partner with God as one of His givers, He in return makes certain that you never run out so that He may continue to use you to give more.

Hinder: Your obedience and your attitude are essential to God's acceptance of your investment in the kingdom.

Genesis 4: 3-9 (*And in process of time it came to pass, that Cain brought of the fruit of the ground an offering unto the LORD. And Abel, he also brought of the firstlings of his flock and of the fat thereof. And the LORD had respect unto Abel and to his offering: But unto Cain and to his offering he had not respect. And Cain was very wroth, and his countenance fell. And the LORD said unto Cain, Why art thou wroth? and why is thy countenance fallen? If thou doest well, shalt thou not be accepted? and if thou doest not well, sin lieth at the door. And unto thee shall be his desire, and thou shalt rule over him. And Cain talked with Abel his brother: and it came to pass, when they were in the field, that Cain rose up against Abel his brother, and slew him. And the LORD said unto Cain, Where is Abel thy brother? And he said, I know not: Am I my brother's keeper?*)

A vital factor to giving is our attitude when we give. Let's look closer at this dynamic in the story of Cain and Abel that I mentioned earlier. Adam and Eve had two sons, Cain, the oldest and Abel, the youngest. God required an offering from them both. It was a specific offering. They were to bring a portion of the best of what they had. Cain was a Cropper and Abel worked as a Shepard. Cain offered God some of the fruit from his harvest. Abel offered God the best of the firstborn lambs from his flock.

The operative word here is "offered". This word does not indicate an automatic acceptance. Therefore God will review their obedience to His request and if they obey, then He will accept the offering; if not then He will reject it. Abel's offering was accepted because he offered God what he asked for. Cain's offering was rejected because he offered less than what was asked. Now, if you read it closely it reads that God had no respect unto Cain or his offering. The attitude behind Cain's offering was that God was not worth his best. God did not like Cain's attitude. He believed that God should be satisfied with what he was giving. It was this type of attitude that led to Cain's disobedience to God. Thus, God rejected him and did not accept his offering. Then Cain becomes angry and God simply says to him, that you have no reason to get angry if you do what I ask.

Abel gave God permission to move in his life by giving. You too can do the same by giving. Nothing leaves heaven until something leaves the earth. You must open your hand and give what's in it and keep it open to receive and even greater return.

NOTES

"Prosperity is a way of living and thinking, and not just money or things. Poverty is a way of living and thinking, and not just a lack of money or things."
~ Eric Butterworth ~

5 Principles of Giving

1) First Fruit

2) Tithe

3) Shepherd's Seed

4) Kingdom Giving

5) **Alms Giving**

Formula: *Acts 20:35* (*I have showed you all things, how that so laboring ye ought to support the weak, and to remember the words of the Lord Jesus, how he said,* **It is more blessed to give than to receive**.)

Giving to those who are less fortunate than we are is called Alms Giving. This form of giving is a private matter and not to be broadcasted or publicized for recognition. Don't give to the less fortunate with the motive of receiving. Give because you have been blessed to give. Don't look for a reward from the person; God will reward you. *Matthew 6:1-4*

I can remember when my wife, Marquita and I were living in Atlanta, Ga. when we first got married. We did not have much. We had very little money and not much furniture or possessions. Almost everything we had could fit in our cars. We were staying in a one bedroom apartment close to the airport. Although, we did not have a lot of things or money we had more than enough love and care for one another to substitute for the stuff. One Saturday afternoon we were sitting on the love seat, which was giving to us by a close friend, watching TV on our 13' screen that sat on the floor. We were hungry because there was no food in our home to eat and no money to buy any. God fixed it so that one of the church members at the church we were attending at the time called and invited us over for dinner. Once we arrived at her home, we shared with her that we were so thankful because we did not have anything to eat. She was so overjoyed that she listened to God and called us over to eat at her home. We had such a fun evening with her and her family eating, laughing and fellowshipping. She even wrapped a lot of food for us to take with us. Marquita and I were thanking and praising God all the way home. The next morning in church our

Pastor changed the normal flow of service and began a testimony service. The woman who had invited us to dinner decided to stand and give her testimony. She began to express how good God was to her. She went further to elaborate on how Minster Williams (me) and his wife didn't have anything to eat and was sitting home hungry with no money. She continued and told how she fed us and gave us leftovers. Needless to say Marquita and I were so embarrassed and humiliated. We had no idea that she was going to announce all of our business to the whole church. At the end of service everyone was hugging her for being such a Good Samaritan. It was devastating for Marquita and me. After this woman was so helpful to us she turned around and unintentionally became so damaging to us.

Give alms from the heart and not to be seen and congratulated by people. God will reward you. For when we do for the less fortunate we do unto God.

Take Action

Note: Now that you have read about Alms Giving, employ what I like to call the "Spirit of Exchange".

The *Spirit of Exchange* is when you take something that you own and give it as a free gift to someone that is unable to reciprocate the gesture. Take time and ask God what he wants you to give. The rule of thumb is if you do not like it or want it then maybe not many others will like or want it. Give away something you would not mind receiving.

Also, seek God for whom to bless with your gift. This gift exchange is not about you. It is about God blessing someone else through you. We are blessed to be a blessing. I am challenging you to make this exchange within a week of reading this portion of the book. You will feel very good about giving. However, resist the temptation of bragging about your act of kindness.

God will surely reward you. I encourage you to share your testimony with the intent to challenge the other person to employ this act of kindness. The *Spirit of Exchange* will become contagious. Make it exciting! You will have joy. People will be helped. God will get the glory and He will gladly allow you to receive the blessings.

Journal

Take a moment and journal your Spirit of Exchange experience.

> "Give yourself entirely to those around you. Be generous with your blessings. A kind gesture can reach a wound that only compassion can heal."
>
> *~ Steve Maraboli ~*

4 Steps to Wealth

1) **Follow the *5 Principles of Giving***

2) **Pay your bills**

Paying your bills is an insignia of one being honest, responsible and a person of integrity. Because we are creatures of habit, paying your bills responsibly should become habitual. Taking care of your regular expenditures should not be an emotional decision or something you do on impulse or spontaneous. So here are a few practical tips to take in consideration regarding this matter.

Create a System for Paying Bills

- ✓ Have a designated area where your financial records are located.
- ✓ Review your statements as soon as they come in.
- ✓ Dispute any discrepancies immediately.
- ✓ Consider online bill pay
- ✓ Make a list of all your bills, how much they are and in order of which they are due.
- ✓ Pay on time and/or before time.

Try and make it a habit to pay more than the minimum payment amount when paying on loans and credit card payments. When doing so, be sure to clearly indicate that you would like for the extra amount you are paying to be accredited to the principal balance.

Create a System to Track your Money

✓ Keep a monthly budget.

I have designed a *Wealth on Purpose Budget* for you to get started. (Budget Spreadsheet Available see p.9).

✓ Record your daily disbursements in a ledger.

By keeping a monthly budget and a ledger it will aide you in recognizing bad spending habits.

✓ Plan your spending for the month.

Try to resist the temptation of accepting invitations to attend various events throughout the month that will cause you to spend outside of your planned budget (e.g. birthday parties, baby showers, galas, dinner etc.). Decline the offer unless you have financially planned for an event or have extra money that is not already ear marked. Proverbs 14:29 *"He who is impulsive exalts folly."*

3) Save and Invest

We are living in a day in time where Social Security and pensions are almost nonexistent. Therefore it behooves every individual to become actively involved in solidifying their own financial future. This action will require purposeful intent. We must not place this concern on the back burner of our affairs. This matter left unresolved will result in endless hardships, stress, sickness and poverty for ourselves at a time when we need help the most. Proverbs 24:33-34 warns that, *"Yet a little sleep, a little slumber, a little folding of the hands to sleep: so shall thy poverty come as one that travelleth; and thy want as an armed man."* So we must not sleep on this, but rather get busy planning for our fiscal imminent now! I will offer more in depth suggestions on saving and investing later in this book. (See *"7 On Purpose Steps"* p.72) For now allow me to propose a few pearls of wisdom to get us started.

✓ Never spend all you have.

Proverbs 21:20 "In the house of the wise are stores of choice food and oil, but a foolish man devours all he has."

- ✓ A savings account has never made anyone rich. You must learn to invest; whether it is stocks, mutual funds, entrepreneurial endeavors, etc.
- ✓ Do not hoard money for fear of not having it. This fear will cause you to make unwise financial decisions.
- ✓ When you are saving money try blocking it out of your mind as if it does not exist. This may help you avoid spending it. It is to be saved not spent.
- ✓ When you invest money you will always run the risk of losing it. You are only guaranteed a sure return when you invest in the Kingdom of God. All other investments are taking a risk.

✓ Refrain from investing too much too quickly. Be diligent in your research of what you are considering to invest in. Start small.

Proverbs 21:5 "The plans of the diligent lead surely to plenty, but those of everyone who is hasty, surely to poverty."

4) Enjoy the rest

Alright, we are finally at the fun part. The reward of working hard is playing hard. An old man once told me that all work and no play makes for a very dull and boring person. Life is short; it is only but a vapor compared to time. Therefore, we must be adamant to seize every moment we can to enjoy it. Enjoying life responsibly is much more exciting than irresponsibly. Being negligent with how you relish life will always end up in regrets and a vast amount of time spent in cleaning up and restoring what was damaged during the false temporary moment of smoke screen pleasure.

God has designed it so that we can have life and enjoy it in abundance, to the full and until it overflows. (John 10:10b AMP) This incentive of life is made possible through the grace and blood shed of Jesus Christ. Thus, since God designed it to be so and Jesus did the work for it to be so, then I need to do my part by partaking in it. It is very simple. Here is how. After you have followed the first three steps to wealth, evaluate what money you have left. This money is free and clear for you to do whatever you like. Go shopping, explore different restaurants, check out the latest movie picture, or even buy a new car. You may say well "I don't have enough money to really enjoy myself like I want to." Not true! You need more creativity than you need money. It is the experience not the cost that is more meaningful.

I can recall one of the most memorable dates my wife and I had. It was about a year before we married. We were both in college with very little money. Marquita was visiting me in my dorm in Atlanta, Ga. from Tallahassee, Fl. It was a Sunday after church and I wanted to do something special for her. I knew all of the guys would be gone from the apartment for a few hours. We used the coffee table to set our food on and we sat on the floor. We ate a gourmet meal made for us by our adopted Godmother who lived in Atlanta as well. After we laughed and ate dinner I took her to the beautiful Piedmont Park. It was such a gorgeous sunny day with perfect comfortable temperature. We talked, laughed, strolled through the park flirting and enjoying one another for hours. She was snacking on a Twinkie and me a small bag of peanuts and water. We experienced the most amazing time together. The total cost for the day was approximately $5.

Have fun and be creative. The more disciplined you are with your money the more money you will have to splurge and explore with. *Ecclesiastes 2:24 There is nothing better for a man than that he should eat and drink and make himself enjoy good in his labor. Even this, I have seen, is from the hand of God.*

8 Laws of Wealth

Law 1: Seed to the sower
Now the One who provides **seed for the sower** and bread for food will provide and multiply your seed and increase the harvest of your righteousness. *2 Corinthians 9:10*

Law 2: Give, and it shall be given unto you
Give, and it shall be given unto you; good measure, pressed down, and shaken together, and running over, shall men give into your bosom. For with the same measure that ye mete withal it shall be measured to you again. *Luke 6:38*

Law 3: You reap what you sow
Remember this: The person who **sows** sparingly will also **reap** sparingly, and the person who sows generously will also reap generously. *2 Corinthians 9:6*

Law 4: Spend to get
Then he that had received the five talents went and traded with the same, and made them other five talents. *Matthew 25:16*

Law 5: Borrower is servant to the lender
The rich rule over the poor, and the **borrower is servant to the lender**. *Proverbs 22:7*

Law 6: Give generously
The wicked borrow and do not repay, but the righteous *give generously* *Psalm 37:21*

Law 7: Only owe love
Let no debt remain outstanding, except the continuing debt to love one another, for he who loves his fellowman has fulfilled the law. *Romans 13:6-8*

Law 8: Be content with what you have
Keep your lives free from the love of money and **be content with what you have**, because God has said, "Never will I leave you; never will I forsake you. *Hebrews 13:5*

7 On Purpose Steps

On Purpose Step 1 - $1,000 Rainy Day Kitty

A rainy day kitty is for those unexpected events where you need quick cash. These events happen suddenly and call for immediate action. For example, a pipe bursts at home, your transmission goes out in the car, or you have to take an emergency trip out of town due to a loved one being sick, etc. No one is exempt from these costly rainy day events from occurring. It is a matter of *when* not if. This rainy day kitty will serve as a buffer to borrowing for such emergencies, which causes you to go deeper in debt. No more borrowing. It's time to break the cycle of debt and poverty!   **START NOW!**

On Purpose Step 2 – 1 by 1 Debt Demolishing System

Create a checklist of your debts. Start with the smallest balance and work your way up to the largest. Don't worry about interest rates unless two debts have similar payoffs. If that's the case, then list the higher interest rate debt first.

The Debt Demolishing System creates momentum by giving you quick and frequent victories. These victories will motivate you to keep going. After a while the large bills will not seem so intimidating any longer. The same amount that you have allotted to pay of the first debt adds to the next debt. Then take those two monthly allotted amounts and add to the next debt. Continue this trend and by the time you reach the larger debts you will be able to tackle it more aggressively.

START NOW!

On Purpose Step 3 - 3 to 6 months Cushion Fund

Determine what it costs for you to live for a total of three to six months. That will serve as the amount to save for your cushion fund. Use the same money that was allotted to pay your debts off in the previous step for this fund. Utilize this money for emergencies only especially, for situations that would cause a decrease in your monthly household income. I recommend that you keep these savings in a money market account.

START NOW!

"Money is like manure, it's only good if you spread it around."

~Winston S. Churchill ~

On Purpose Step 4 - Invest

Congratulations, by now you should have no payments (except the house) and a fully funded rainy day kitty. Now we want to work on creating extra streams of income and becoming aggressive about our retirement fund. Research and find a business, stock or personal venture that you can invest in. Start small and work your way up. It would be foolish to invest all of your extra money. In addition, I recommend investing no less than 10% of your household income into Roth IRAs and pre-tax retirement plans.

START NOW!

On Purpose Step 5 – College fund for children

Attaining a college degree is possible without having to acquire loans. Set a goal that would adequately satisfy the money needed for college. Determine how much per month you should be saving at 12% interest in order to have enough for college. If you save at 12% and inflation is at 4%, then you are moving ahead of inflation at a net of 8% per year! I recommend using Education Savings Accounts (ESAs) and 529 plans to save for college. **START NOW!**

On Purpose Step 6 – Burn the mortgage

You still have extra money but don't quite look at it as extra yet. We will call it unmarked money instead. Use this money to aggressively pay off your mortgage early. You have built up a massive force of momentum so don't slow down now. You are just about at the dream of having no debt. *Romans 13:6-8* **START NOW!**

On Purpose Step 7 – Be a blessing

You are now living in abundance. Allow God to use you to bless others. Be generous because giving as God leads can never deplete you. God always gives back more than what we give. Also, be certain to leave an inheritance for your family.

Be careful not to get all you can, can all you get and then sit on the can. Vow to never hold your money so tightly that you never give any away. Hoarding money is a sign of fear. Giving is a sign of faith.

START NOW!

> "Money is like a sixth sense –
> and you can't make use of
> the other five without it."
>
> ~ William Somerset
> Maugham ~

Testimonials

My wife, Beverly and I, are two former crack addicts as well as former U.S. Postal workers who were terminated in the late 80's. Back then, if you worked for the Post Office you were considered as having a "premium" job. During this time we were considered what was called "functioning addicts' meaning we would smoke drugs and get high but still go to work when we were supposed to, but pay day was a different story altogether. We had a slogan we used for our Friday pay days - "money in hand, change in plan".

We would spend practically every penny of our paychecks and be broke on Saturday. This vicious cycle went on for quite some time until we both eventually were terminated from our company. No one believed that we would ever overcome our addictions or have any material things of life again. But thanks to the prayers of our mothers, and many others, God was still working in our lives.

The first time I heard the terms "First Fruits" and "Shepherd's Seed" was after I had become a member of Life Church International. Pastor J was teaching on these topics and I know it had to be God that led me there because my purpose for going was to stop my wife from going, which she had already become a member.

However, all that changed once I stepped inside the doors of the sanctuary. I was greeted with much love and affection. I was unemployed at the time, and Pastor J taught a message entitled "Better". Shortly after that I was re-hired by the company that fired me. Then came the message "Prepare for the Rain", which made me feel like he was speaking directly to me. That caused me to step out on faith and start my very own trucking business.

The next teaching that came was "Learning How to Hear from God". During this teaching the church was put on a fast and I believe God spoke to me to expand the business and for us to purchase a second truck. Shortly after that, I got confirmation by way of my wife being terminated from her job of 18 years. Then, immediately the second truck was purchased with only half of what used to be a two income household. God's still working!

Now comes the teaching of "First Fruits" and "Shepherd's Seed", where Pastor J taught us how the Levites took care of the Shepherd with the first fruits of their harvest to cover them for the remainder of the year. This started as a struggle in our flesh because it was also time to file our taxes, and we had not put any money aside if we had to pay the IRS.

We decided that we were going to be obedient to God and the teachings and pay our first fruits, which was a huge sacrifice. We got our taxes filed, and not only did we not have to pay, but we got a tremendous blessing of a $21,000.00 refund. God's principles of Tithing, Offerings, First Fruits, and Shepherd's Seed are for our benefit that truly work and are available to anyone who is willing to apply the principles. There is no pit too low that

God can't raise you up and out of. To God be the Glory.

In His service,

Howard Hooper

Hello Pastor J!

I am writing to share my progress and testimony regarding the 5 principles of giving. First, I just want to say, I thank God for leading me to Life Church international. You, Lady M and the whole LCI Family have been a blessing to me and my family.

Well, I have been tithing for a while. However, my overall attitude regarding giving has changed and that's a testimony in itself. My biggest issue was with First Fruits. I was nervous because the amount of one week's pay is well more than I have ever given at one time. Even though I felt that way, I said with my mouth that I choose to Trust GOD in my finances knowing that some kind of way all my needs will be met. So, I set my mind to make sure I just take the money out and put it straight into the envelope and seal it. In the same week, a series of things began to happen.

1. An overflow of loans hit our department, my manager personally asked me to work extra hours even though I didn't qualify yet because I was new. So, even after the first fruit seed I had money for my bills.

2. At the beginning of the school year, my oldest son Tony was denied the grant for free tutoring services, so I have been looking for a company that provides tutoring for a reasonable price. I was planning to start tutoring services this week. But one day during

lunch I was checking my voicemail and got a message from a tutoring company that says they were calling because they got information from Duval County Schools to start tutoring Tony. So Tony has free tutoring for at least 90 days from the same company that gave me a rate of $40.00 an hour.

3. Recently, I became a Florida Notary. God opened the door for me to be the personal notary for a tax company. I only go there once a week for no more than 2 hours. For the past 2 weeks, I have made more in those couple hours than I do in a whole days work on my job and I just say Thank You Jesus, for providing all my needs and above my needs.

I am learning to trust GOD in all things and I know he will give me the wisdom I need to succeed in every area. My motivational scripture:

Philippians 3:13 Brethren, I count not myself to have apprehended: but [this] one thing [I do], forgetting those things which are behind, and reaching forth unto those things which are before, 14 I press toward the mark for the prize of the high calling of God in Christ Jesus.

Thank you,

Chauna S. White

Faithfulness Pays Off

Greetings Pastor J,

My husband and I have been applying the **Wealth On Purpose** principles and I would like to share with you a few things that God has done for me and my family. We began our journey here in Jacksonville in January 2007. I was fired from a job 3 months prior in September of 2006 (two days before our wedding day) and did not find work until February 2007. We stayed in a room in a relative's home for a few months before God opened the door for us to purchase our own home in April. August came around and I was told that because of budget cuts I could not return to work and due to financial difficulty at my husband's place of employment his pay suffered greatly. We did not know how we were going to eat day to day, how we were going to get our lights back on or how we were going to get around the city with little to no gas. Not to mention, our laundry and my hair was needed a relaxer, badly!!! We did not have air conditioning for the first few years of being in our new home. The summer months were difficult. We struggled for months until I was able to find temporary employment in October. Soon after, God provided me with permanent employment in February of 2008. I remained employed with this company until September 2012. I was stressed and bitter the majority of my tenure there. My hair was falling out, and the position I worked in was very stressful.

Nevertheless, throughout all of our struggles my husband and I NEVER turned our backs on God. We were in church faithfully, even when we didn't really want to be there. We served the church and others faithfully. We trusted and believed that God would bring us out of these day to day struggles. We continued to give of ourselves and whatever we possessed because we believed that if we continued to give-not grudgingly- that our hands would remain open for God to place blessings within them. Even though we did not have much we gave what we had. We paid our tithe from whatever came into our hands. God placed people in our lives to bless us at our lowest and darkest times. Even some people who schemed and plotted against us to keep us down God used them to bless us, his children.

Pastor, God has given you many sermons to share with us that have truly helped my husband and I understand him more. The instructions were so clear. They were simple and we knew that they would only be hard to follow if we just refused to follow them. The 5 Principles of Giving and the 7 On Purpose Steps that God gave you to give to us at Life Church helped us and has been helping us become debt free and live in **Wealth on Purpose**. They have blessed us so....we have been applying these principles and denying our flesh (most of the time) and we have shared the messages with others and so far:

1. I have been blessed with a great paying career that embodies my occupation desires

2. My children have schools that are both affordable & dependable with one year free tuition

3. My children are healthy and are now covered with an affordable insurance plan

4. My husband has been accepted into a program that will award him access to a career of his goals as an addition to his successful business he runs.

5. We received an unexpected lump sum check in the mail

6. Much of our debt has been demolished! We have a student loan and our house note remaining....

With love and appreciation,

Lisa

I recently finished teaching on Alms Giving and I was shopping in a department store a few weeks later. I found some of the best sales and bargains on the few items I purchased. As I approached the counter to check out I read the name tag of the clerk that would assist me. She looked to be at least in her late fifties or early sixties.

"Hi Cindy, how are you today?" I said.

She replies, "Well I'm here, how are you"? We continued small talk, but her first reply, 'Well I'm here' made me tune in to our conversation a little more it caused me to become concerned. To lighten the conversation I joked with Cindy saying that my wife says I'm cheap.

Cindy said with a smile, "Next time tell her you are not cheap you just cut corners to have more money left over to spend on her." we both laughed.

Suddenly her demeanor changed and her facial expression dropped. She talked about how she had been married twice and she was done with believing in marriage altogether. Consequently, she encouraged her daughter not to get married to her boyfriend that she is living with and has been dating for the last five years. She went as far as to advice her daughter to have children with him but not to marry him.

Cindy continued talking about how she has four children from her first husband. She said he treated so badly when they were married. She remembered how he expected her to keep the floors scrubbed, food prepared and on the table by six o'clock every night; take care of the children, work and take care of him. She was to do all of this with no help from him. She would ask her husband to help with the kids and he would snap at her and reply, "You wanted these kids so you take care of them!"

Even more disturbing she explained how her children were all grown now and she just exists now. She mentioned that she only goes to work and goes home. Cindy also stated, she now lives with her daughter because no one else wants to be bothered. To me she seemed depressed and bitter. So I asked her what advice she could give me for my marriage. She admonished me to show my wife that I care and consider her. Cindy urged me to buy my wife a card or flowers ever so often for no other reason but to show her you were thinking about her. "Those small acts of kindness go along way and can really brighten up her day." she counseled. I said, "Thank you and enjoy the rest of your day."

As I walked off, another customer approached Cindy's register. The customer asked how she was today and Cindy again replied with a smile, "Well, I'm here." God began to speak to my spirit to do something nice for Cindy in order that He may minister to her. I heard the spirit instruct me to take the same advice she gave me for my wife and use it to brighten Cindy's day. I thought to buy her a card and give her a seed of $50. I honestly did not want to do anything but pray for her and move on. God would not allow this thought to leave me alone so I asked my wife if she was okay with me doing this for this woman. My wife was elated with the idea. Here is what the card read.

Hi Cindy, I was in your store the other day, we spoke briefly and you gave me great wisdom on how to be a better husband to my wife. I wanted to get you this card to say thank you. I noticed that you may be facing rough time in your life now, but things will get better for you. Be careful not to rely on any man for your happiness because every person in your life will disappoint you in some way. The only person who will never disappoint you is Jesus. I do not know if you know Him or not but if not please get to know him because He loves you more than you love yourself. Never stop smiling, it allows the light into your soul.

I placed the fifty dollars in the card along with my business card, just in case she wanted to get in touch with me to learn more about Christ or just to say thank you. I went by the store to drop the card off. I left it with one of her co-workers while she was on break. I did not want to really carry on a great conversation so I left. I knew this act of kindness was not about me I needed only to be obedient to God. It has been over two months since I did this and I have not received a response from Cindy, but God honored my obedience. Two weeks after I left the card my wife and I received an unexpected check in the mail for the amount of seventeen hundred dollars. God honored our obedience to him because we followed the principles of Alms Giving.

P.S. My wife and I remain in prayer for Cindy.

Signed:

Pastor J Marcellas Williams

A Mother's Love

For about two years, my family and I have been faithful disciples of Life Church International. When Pastor J. initially began teaching the **"Wealth On Purpose"** series, I did not start applying the principles he taught. As I began to grow more I started applying the principles; my children and I *began seeing a difference in our finances*. My eleven year old son Kristopher, a fifth grade safety patrol officer at Martin Luther King Jr. Elementary School, really took notice. Each year, the school's safety patrols take a trip to Washington DC to tour the monuments and see the sites. They also take a trip to Busch Gardens in Tampa at the end of the year. The total cost of these trips comes to $632.00, not including money for food and expenditures.

Now, I'm a single parent and I'm not making that much on my job to be able to come up with this type of money by the end of the year, because I have bills and other pressing matters. However, I thought to myself, 'this is a once in a life time trip!' What could I do to help my child? How could I come up with money, the right way and not the wrong way? Surprisingly, Kristopher came to me and said, "Mama, what would Pastor J say?" So, I replied "you're right!" Then, he said to me, "Mama, can you ask Pastor J would it be ok for me to sale some items after church to raise my funds for my trip?" I told him I would and so, I did. Pastor J permitted us to start selling. So every Sunday my son would go out in front of the church and sell his snack items. He was out there no matter what; in the hot sun, the cold wind, and sometimes in the dripping rain trying to raise the money for his trip.

During the weeks that Pastor J was teaching the **'Wealth On Purpose'** series, I instilled into Kristopher the principles and *he followed those steps*, including paying his tithe every week from the money he made by selling the snack items [Tithe]. He gave a seed offering toward the Life City Vision [Kingdom Giving]. Furthermore, he gave Pastor J, his wife and kids a bag full of chips, sodas, and candy every week for free [Sheppard's Seed]. All the while he was faithful, being a good steward to his candy store. Pastor J had spoken to Kristopher and told him that he would give $100 of his own money to help toward his trip. Well, Kristopher remembered what Pastor J spoke about giving and being a blessing to others. It just so happened that there was another child at Life Church who was also a safety patrol officer, yet, at a different school, and they wanted to also raise funds for the same trip. My son graciously stepped aside to let the other child sell snack items so that this child could gain as much support as he did [Alms Giving]. What an awesome gesture of Godly love and being a blessing to others. Pastor J, however remembered his promise to Kristopher and one Sunday he told the church our story. Just as he finished telling the story Pastor J pulled out the $100 that he had previously told Kristopher he would give him. He then, asks the other members to sow a seed into Kristopher for his trip. With that being said, *my son is debt free!!* He paid for his trip and was blessed with *overflow*: spending money for his trip.

Hallelujah! This is something that we are totally thankful for. Generosity never goes unnoticed! Kristopher was faithful to God, LCI, and his store and *God returned the faithfulness with interest!!* Kris now wants to sale the rest of his snack items and donate the money from those sales to the youth department at the LCI to go towards the 'Back 2 School' supplies. I am a very proud mother of a kindhearted young man. As long as he keeps listening to the word of God that is being taught through our pastor, Pastor J. Marcellas Williams, and applying these principles and 'Living On Purpose', my son will make it even further than my mind can imagine. He will experience **'Wealth On Purpose'**!

Proud Mother,
Randesha Brown

Kristopher tells the story in his own words:

I started raising money for my safety patrol trip, so I can go to DC and see lots of cool things. With the help of Pastor J and my employee cousins Crystal, Man Man (Christian), and Lil Man (Chrishon), I was raising funds every week. Some weeks slower than others but, that was ok. I know why I was out there and that was to raise my own money without asking anyone for it. There was a girl in the church that was a safety patrol too who wanted to raise some money as well; I stopped selling so she can reach her goal. I started back selling to finish out my goal. I at least wanted to raise $500. I raise the whole $632.00 and spending cash with the Help of Pastor J donating $100.00 and the church sowing a seed into me to help me pay for my trip. I now have spending money even with my tithe being paid. I'm still covered by the blood of Jesus. I'm so grateful for everything and the members of my church. I thank everyone and I'm really thankful for Pastor J for being there for me and allowing me to open my candy store. I think I'm ready to open up my own little business..... *Sincerely Kristopher Brown*

The Prayer

Father, I pray for my friend who has taken time to immerse themselves in this teaching. Cause Your Holy Spirit to illuminate for them what You are speaking to them personally. I thank You that as they apply these principles they will experience life better than ever before. Make it so that they are not only blessed but are also a blessing to others. Thank You, God that peace and endless joy will find their dwelling place in the daily life of my dear friend.

I pray that favor will chase you down and over take every endeavor you put your hands to do. You, your offspring and others who are connected to you shall lack for nothing all the days of your life. You shall dream and see vision again to behold the fulfillment and manifestation, in Jesus' name, Amen.

NOTES

www.ingramcontent.com/pod-product-compliance
Lightning Source LLC
Chambersburg PA
CBHW041146210326
41519CB00046B/138